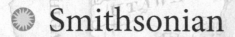

Smithsonian

T0040574

Exploring
the
Massachusetts
Colony

by Danielle Smith-Llera

CAPSTONE PRESS
a capstone imprint

Smithsonian books are published by Capstone Press,
1710 Roe Crest Drive, North Mankato, Minnesota 56003
www.capstonepub.com

Library of Congress Cataloging-in-Publication Data
Names: Smith-Llera, Danielle, 1971–author.
Title: Exploring the Massachusetts Colony / by Danielle Smith-Llera.
Description: North Mankato, Minnesota: Capstone Press, [2017]
 Series: Smithsonian. Exploring the 13 Colonies | Includes bibliographical references and index.
Audience: Ages 8–11.
Identifiers: LCCN 2016008183
ISBN 9781515722373 (library binding)
ISBN 9781515722502 (paperback)
ISBN 9781515722632 (ebook PDF)
Subjects: LCSH: Massachusetts—History—Colonial period, ca. 1600–1775—Juvenile literature.
Massachusetts—History—1775–1865—Juvenile literature.
Classification: LCC F67 .S67 2017 | DDC 974.4/02—dc23
LC record available at http://lccn.loc.gov/2016008183

Editorial Credits
Jennifer Huston, editor; Richard Parker, designer; Eric Gohl, media researcher;
Kathy McColley, production specialist

Our very special thanks to Stephen Binns at the Smithsonian Center for Learning and Digital Access for
his curatorial review. Capstone would also like to thank Kealy Gordon, Smithsonian Institution Product
Development Manager, and the following at Smithsonian Enterprises: Christopher A. Liedel, President;
Carol LeBlanc, Senior Vice President; Brigid Ferraro, Vice President; Ellen Nanney, Licensing Manager.

Photo Credits
Alamy: 19th Era, 23 (top); Bridgeman Images: Peter Newark American Pictures/Private Collection,
37; Capstone: 4; Courtesy of Army Art Collection, U.S. Army Center of Military History: 39; David R.
Wagner: 9; Getty Images: Bettmann, 21 (bottom), Stock Montage, 16, 31; Granger, NYC: 6, 8, 17; Library
of Congress: 18, 33, 38; Newscom: Picture History, 26, Prisma, 30; New York Public Library: 27; North
Wind Picture Archives: cover, 7, 10, 11, 12, 13, 14, 19 (all), 20, 21 (top), 23 (bottom), 25, 28, 29, 32, 34, 35,
40; Shutterstock: f11photo, 41; Wikimedia: Public Domain, 5, 15, 36

Design Elements: Shutterstock

Table of Contents

Introduction:

The 13 Colonies

In the early 1600s, many people left Europe in the hopes of creating new and better lives. They crossed the Atlantic Ocean to establish colonies in North America. A colony is a place settled by people from another country. But the colonists were not free to govern themselves. They had to follow the laws of their home country. By the early 1700s, England had set up 13 Colonies along the eastern coast of the present-day United States.

The English were not the first people to build homes and communities in North America. In fact they were not even the first Europeans to set foot on the eastern coast of North America. But these 13 Colonies would eventually join together to become the United States of America.

Bartholomew Gosnold was one of the first Europeans to explore what is now Massachusetts. He named Cape Cod for the plentiful fish he found there.

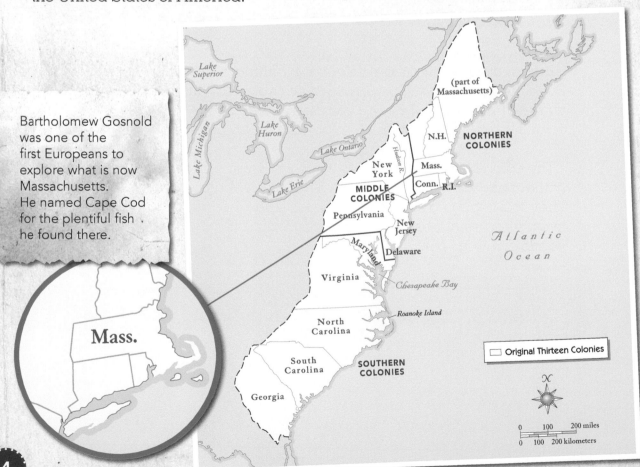

Scrambling for a Piece of the New World

In the 1400s Europeans were looking to find easier ways to sail to Asia. They had to sail east for months to bring back rich cargoes of spices, fine silks, and delicate pottery. In 1492 Spain sent Italian explorer Christopher Columbus on a voyage to reach Asia by sailing west across the Atlantic Ocean. At the time nobody knew that other continents blocked the way. When Columbus landed on islands near present-day Florida, he claimed the land for Spain.

Another explorer discovered the northern part of North America by accident too. In 1497 John Cabot left England aboard a small ship with 18 men. He landed in what is now Canada and claimed the cold, northern region for England.

Early explorers failed to reach Asia by sailing west, but the lands they did find captured the imagination of Europeans. They dreamed of starting new lives or finding gold in this "New World." Adventurers from Spain, England, France, Portugal, and the Netherlands returned from the New World with tales of lands rich in **natural resources**. English businessmen saw this as an opportunity to make money. By the 1500s England's government was planning to **colonize** the New World. This would make England richer and more powerful.

Christopher Columbus (wearing red and raising flag) and his crew arrived off the coast of North America on October 12, 1492.

natural resource—something in nature that people use, such as coal and trees

colonize— to formally settle a new territory

Early English Settlements

Setting up new colonies was an enormous challenge. In 1587 English **immigrants** tried to establish a colony on an island off the coast of present-day North Carolina. But the colonists mysteriously disappeared after less than three years.

In 1602 another group led by English explorer Bartholomew Gosnold built a fort on an island off the coast of what is now Massachusetts. But they abandoned it when they feared running out of supplies and having conflicts with Native Americans. Finally, in 1607, Virginia became the first permanent English colony in North America.

Why They Came

People had many different reasons for crossing an ocean to begin a new life. Some immigrants hoped to get rich off the land.

Before there was even a permanent English colony in North America, Bartholomew Gosnold (center, in green) traded with Native Americans in what is now Massachusetts.

Others wanted to escape difficult lives in Europe. Some were looking for freedom to practice their religion. In England at the time, people were punished if they didn't belong to the Church of England—the nation's official church. Those who refused to join the Church of England had to pay fines or go to jail. At least one man had an ear cut off for following his own faith. The colonies of Massachusetts, Rhode Island, Maryland, and Pennsylvania were all founded by people seeking religious freedom.

English people who didn't follow the Church of England faced fines and punishment. The people shown here left England to live in the New World where they could practice their religion without being punished.

Coming to the New World filled immigrants with hope as well as fear. They spent months crossing the dangerous ocean. When they finally arrived, they worried about finding food and shelter. Yet they risked their lives, trying to build a better future for themselves and their families.

The Original 13 Colonies

The first permanent European settlement in each colony:

Virginia	1607	Delaware	1638
Massachusetts	**1620**	Pennsylvania	1643
New Hampshire	1623	North Carolina	1653
New York	1624	New Jersey	1660
Connecticut	1633	South Carolina	1670
Maryland	1634	Georgia	1733
Rhode Island	1636		

immigrant—a person who moves from one country to live permanently in another

Chapter 1:
Native People of Massachusetts

When the first settlers arrived in Massachusetts, they found people already living there. The region was home to several Native American tribes, including the Wampanoag and Massachusett tribes. These tribes were all part of the Algonquian group and they spoke the same language. The Algonquian tribes traded goods and protected each other from enemies.

Life in an Algonquian Village

Inside tribal villages everyone worked together to help the village survive. Each season villagers moved to where food was plentiful. They could easily take apart their wigwams—dome-shaped homes constructed from bent sticks and bark. In the spring they moved closer to the coast. Men caught salmon and cod with spears and nets while women collected shellfish, such as oysters and clams. A dead whale on the shore meant plenty of food for a feast. During the summer women tended gardens of corn, beans, and squash. Children pulled weeds and chased animals away from the crops.

Native Americans of the Northeast typically pulled injured or dead whales to the shore.

The Native Americans were skilled at growing corn and other crops. They taught the first settlers how to grow these crops, which helped the newcomers to survive.

In the winter tribes moved into the forests. Men carved arrowheads out of stone, bones, and antlers. They hunted deer, bears, turkeys, and even skunks with bows and arrows. They dried some of the meat so they could store it to eat later.

The women collected berries and nuts in handwoven baskets. For cooking they used homemade clay pots, which sat on stones over a fire. The women also ground corn and made it into cornbread.

The Native Americans used every part of the animals they caught for food, clothing, or shelter. Deerskins provided clothing year-round. In warmer months men and older children wore aprons with flaps around the waist called "breechcloths." Women wore skirts. In colder months they added leggings and leather shirts to keep warm.

Tribe members were grateful to nature's plants and animals for providing food and shelter. They thanked the spirits of any animals they killed during the hunt. They celebrated harvests with dancing and wearing their finest clothing, feathers, and body paint.

Women taught girls to cook, sew, and make pottery. Men taught boys to hunt and carve tools and weapons. Older tribe members told stories to teach children the traditions of their **ancestors**. One favorite story described how a kind giant shaped their coastal land with his feet.

Tribe members also participated in their government. At village gatherings people discussed solutions to problems. The chiefs did not make decisions without gathering advice from tribal **council** members.

On special occasions Native Americans, such as the Wampanoag warrior shown here, wore body paint and headdresses made of feathers.

Trade and Tragedy

Tribes often traded with each other, sometimes using wampum—beads carved from clamshells. To the tribes wampum was more valuable than money.

The Native Americans traded with Europeans long before colonies were founded in present-day Massachusetts. Since the 1500s, ships carrying fur traders and fishermen sailed the area's coast and rivers. Tribe members traded their furs for brass kettles. By cutting up the metal, they fashioned sharp points for their weapons and new pieces of jewelry.

But this trade also brought disaster to tribes in the area. Europeans carried **smallpox**, measles, and other diseases. These diseases were new to the Native Americans. By 1620 the Wampanoag and Massachusett tribes had been reduced from more than 12,000 people to only around 2,000.

After Europeans arrived in North America, many Native Americans died of smallpox and other diseases.

ancestor—a family member who lived a long time ago
council—a group of people elected to make decisions for a larger group
smallpox—a disease that spreads easily from person to person, causing chills, fever, and pimples that scar

Chapter 2:
Making a New Life

In 1614 Captain John Smith, founder of the Jamestown settlement in Virginia, explored the coasts of Massachusetts and Maine by boat. In 1616 he published a detailed map of this area, which he called "New England."

In 1620 a group of people set sail from England on the *Mayflower* on their way to America. These people, now called the "Pilgrims," were known as "Separatists" because they broke away from the Church of England. They were willing to risk their lives to settle in a place where they could practice their religion in peace.

Many of the Pilgrims had already fled England and had been living in the Netherlands. There the Pilgrims were allowed to practice their religion freely, but it was difficult to find jobs. They also worried that their children would forget their English culture.

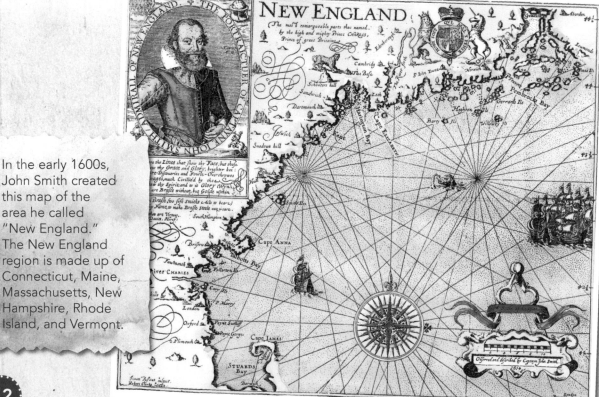

In the early 1600s, John Smith created this map of the area he called "New England." The New England region is made up of Connecticut, Maine, Massachusetts, New Hampshire, Rhode Island, and Vermont.

With the Mayflower anchored off shore, the Pilgrims arrived at Plymouth Rock in what is now Massachusetts in mid-November 1620.

The *Mayflower* Sets Sail

The Pilgrims risked everything to get to the New World. They sold most of their belongings and crowded onto the *Mayflower* in September 1620. The journey was not easy for the 102 passengers, including about 30 children. Supplies began running out during the long ocean voyage.

The Pilgrims had planned to land near the Hudson River in present-day New York, but strong storms blew them off course. Instead they made landfall further north at Cape Cod in what is now Massachusetts. After exploring the area for a while, they decided to stay. On the mainland across Cape Cod Bay from where they'd landed, they founded Plymouth in December 1620. Plymouth became the second permanent English colony in North America. But with winter's arrival, the future of the exhausted, hungry colonists looked grim.

Challenges at the Plymouth Colony

The Pilgrims were grateful for the freshwater they found in the ponds and streams nearby. They even found farm fields that Native Americans had abandoned. But the Pilgrims had no horses or cows and only hand tools for farming.

The winter was deadly for the unprepared Pilgrims. Nearly half of them died from disease and starvation. They buried their companions without markers so nearby tribes would not know how defenseless they were.

The Pilgrims were unprepared for the snow and cold weather they experienced during their first winter in North America. Many did not survive.

Hope for the Young Colony

In the spring some Native Americans walked into the small settlement and offered help. One of them, a Wampanoag named Squanto, became a close friend to the desperate colonists.

Squanto made it possible for the Plymouth colonists to survive. He taught them how to plant crops, catch fish, and gather wild plants to eat. He also taught them how to bury dead fish as **fertilizer** to make the soil better for growing crops.

Critical Thinking with Primary Sources

Many historians consider the Mayflower Compact the first written framework for government in America. Why do you think the *Mayflower* passengers felt it was important to put this agreement in writing? How can you tell that the signers wanted a democratic government where people could vote to make decisions and elect leaders?

"We ... combine ourselves together into a civil Body Politick, for our better Ordering and Preservation ... And by Virtue hereof do enact ... such just and equal Laws, Ordinances, Acts, Constitutions, and Officers, from time to time, as shall be thought most ... convenient for the general Good of the Colony."

In October 1621 the Pilgrims and Wampanoags celebrated the harvest and their friendship with a great feast. This is often referred to as the first Thanksgiving.

A New Government

When the Pilgrims came ashore in America, they brought with them a historic document. The Mayflower Compact was a plan for government that was written during the long ocean voyage. Many passengers had signed the document while at sea. William Bradford, one of the signers, became governor of the Plymouth Colony. He managed the colony's laws and courts. He also worked to keep peace and trade flowing with nearby tribes.

fertilizer—a substance added to soil to make crops grow better

New Arrivals

In 1630 a fleet of 12 ships carrying about 1,000 people left England for Massachusetts. Like the Pilgrims these **Puritans** wanted to practice their religion without fear of punishment. But unlike the Pilgrims, the Puritans didn't plan to separate from the Church of England. They just wanted to change or "purify" it.

When the Puritans arrived in North America, they carried with them a **charter** from England's King Charles I. The charter said they could build a colony between the Charles and Merrimack Rivers. John Winthrop, the group's leader, wanted to establish a fair, hardworking, and faithful community. He hoped it would be an example to England—and to the world—of the value of Puritan beliefs.

After two months at sea, Winthrop and the Puritans made landfall at present-day Salem, Massachusetts. They left Salem after a few weeks and traveled south, searching for a good place with a source of freshwater. They finally settled near the mouth of the Charles River. They established the Massachusetts Bay Colony and named their new town Boston after the English hometown of several colonists.

John Winthrop (1588–1649)

Born in Suffolk County, England, John Winthrop was deeply religious, but he was troubled by what he saw as problems with the Church of England. However, because the King of England was the head of the **Anglican** Church, criticizing it meant breaking the law. When Winthrop lost his government job because of his Puritan beliefs, he decided to make a fresh start in America.

Winthrop joined the Massachusetts Bay Company, which elected him governor of their new colony. Winthrop believed that only strict rules could keep the community in order. Not everyone agreed, but Winthrop's followers respected him and elected him governor 12 times.

The Colony Takes Off

About 200 people from the Massachusetts Bay Colony died during their first winter in America. But the colonists did not give up. In fact in the 1630s, during what is known as the "Great Migration," more than 20,000 immigrants moved to Massachusetts. These new colonists brought a steady supply of much-needed goods, such as cookware, clothing, and guns. Over time local shops and businesses were established in Boston, and the city quickly grew.

English settlements also spread outside of Boston, including the towns of Charlestown, Dorchester, and Roxbury. In the years to come, new colonies were founded in nearby Rhode Island, New Hampshire, and farther away in Connecticut and New York.

In 1634 the Puritans purchased the land now known as the Boston Common, which was then used as a grazing area for livestock. In the 1830s the Boston Common became America's first public park.

> "[W]e must consider that we shall be as a city upon a hill. The eyes of all people are upon us."
>
> —John Winthrop in a speech given on the ship *Arabella* during the 1630 journey to America

Puritan—a follower of a strict religion common during the 1500s and 1600s. Puritans wanted simple church services and enforced a strict moral code.

charter—an official document granting permission to set up a new colony, organization, or company

Anglican—relating to the Church of England

Chapter 3:
Daily Life in Massachusetts

Massachusetts' first colonists worked hard just to survive. Farming was difficult because the soil along the Atlantic coast was full of sand and rocks. Plus winter brought many months of ice and heavy snow. Still, the colonists were determined to build their "city on a hill."

A Simple Life

Winthrop and other Puritan leaders instructed their followers to live simple lives with few distractions from work and prayer. The Puritans mostly wore plain, drab colors, and they avoided the lace collars, gold thread, and satin fabric popular in England at the time. Instead they wore simple linen or wool clothing. Puritan women covered their hair with bonnets. In contrast fashionable European women wore flashy feathers, ribbons, and even jewels in their hair.

Puritan homes were just as simple with no fancy furniture from England inside. Often, very large families—some with 10 or more children—crammed into houses with only two rooms. Puritan men initially built homes like the ones they'd left in England. Logs and clay formed the walls and grass covered the roofs. They sat on wooden benches or stools.

Puritan women wore simple clothing and hats to cover their bodies as much as possible.

The Meetinghouse

Puritan homes were built around the meetinghouse—the most important building in town. Townspeople gathered inside for meetings. Only white men who owned property and attended church could vote and elect leaders.

Church was the center of Puritan life and services could last for hours at a time.

A Life of Prayer and Study

The meetinghouse was also the church. For Puritans religion was so important that people were forbidden to work on Sunday. Women were not even allowed to cook on Sundays, so they prepared meals the day before.

Inside the meetinghouse Puritans prayed, sang songs, and listened to sermons for hours. During services a long pole was used to poke sleeping adults and misbehaving children.

People who missed church had to pay a fine. Some were even shamed in public. They had to stand in the town square with their head and hands trapped in a torture device called a **pillory**. If they broke major rules, they could have their skin branded with burning hot irons.

In Colonial times, pillories were used to publicly shame people and punish them for crimes.

pillory—a device formerly used for publicly punishing wrongdoers consisting of a wooden frame with holes in which the head and hands can be locked

A Day in the Life

Every man, woman, and child worked to help their family survive. Men and boys hunted and fished. They also worked outside planting crops and chopping wood.

Women worked together growing peas, beans, and squash in community gardens. They cooked stews in pots hanging inside the kitchen fireplace. They dried herbs, vegetables, and meat to eat during cold months. Women taught their daughters to knead bread, sew, and use a spinning wheel to make wool thread.

Puritans believed everyone should read the Bible, which meant everyone needed to know how to read. Even girls were taught to read, which was not common in England at the time.

The Massachusetts Bay Colony had a law requiring all towns with more than 50 families to have a public school. The Boston Latin School, which was established in 1635, was America's first public school. It is still educating students today.

This Puritan woman reads her Bible while spinning wool into thread.

In Adam's fall We sinned all.	As runs the Glass, Man's life doth pass.	Nightingales sing In time of spring.	Time cuts down all, Both great and small.
Thy life to mend, God's Book attend.	My book and Heart Shall never part.	The royal Oak, it was the tree That saved his royal majesty.	Uriah's beauteous wife Made David seek his life.
The Cat doth play, And after slay.	Job feels the rod, Yet blesses God.	Peter denies His Lord, and cries.	Whales in the sea God's voice obey.
A Dog will bite A thief at night.	Proud Korah's troop Was swallowed up.	Queen Esther comes in royal state, To save the Jews from dismal fate.	Xerxes the Great did die, And so must you and I.
The Eagle's flight Is out of sight.	The Lion bold The Lamb doth hold.	Rachel doth mourn For her first-born.	Youth forward slips— Death soonest nips.
The idle Fool Is whipped at school.	The Moon gives light In time of night.	Samuel anoints Whom God appoints.	Zaccheus, he Did climb the tree, His Lord to see.

For more than 150 years, the *New England Primer* taught children in early America to read.

In smaller towns young boys and girls would gather in a teacher's house to study. Students learned to read, write, and do basic math. Many children in Massachusetts and other colonies studied the *New England Primer*, a book first published in Boston in 1688. It used prayers, poems, and Bible passages to teach children to read.

Critical Thinking with Primary Sources

In Colonial times, children from smaller towns learned to read and write in a teacher's home. These were called "dame schools." Children would bring things to the teacher as payment, such as an apple or a piece of wood for the fire. Examine this painting of a dame school in Colonial New England. What things do these children have in their classroom that you do not? What things do you have in your classroom that they do not? Do you think it was easier or more difficult to learn in Colonial times?

Most public schools were only for boys. Some boys went to study with a master craftsman instead. They learned how to become blacksmiths, shoemakers, or cabinetmakers. Girls learned to weave cloth, sew dresses, or make candles.

A few young men went on to further study at Harvard University. Established in 1636, it is the oldest university in the United States.

A Colony Just for Puritans

Although they came to America seeking religious freedom, Puritan leaders made it illegal to practice any other religion in Massachusetts. But minister Roger Williams believed that people should have the freedom to practice any religion they choose. This angered Governor Winthrop and the colony's religious leaders.

The Great Awakening (1734–1750)

In the 1730s some religious leaders worried that church was not as important to colonists as it once was. Preachers such as Jonathan Edwards and George Whitefield gave emotion-filled speeches to scare listeners into reading their Bibles. This was known as the "Great Awakening." The preachers wanted Christians to focus on developing a personal relationship with God rather than following strict church rituals. An enthusiastic crowd of 25,000 people once filled Boston Common to hear Whitefield preach. People flocked to Edwards' church in Northampton or read his printed sermons. From 1734 to 1750, preachers like Edwards and Whitefield encouraged people across the 13 Colonies to return to religion.

Did You Know?

Eight U.S. presidents have graduated from Harvard. They are John Adams, John Quincy Adams, Rutherford Hayes, Theodore Roosevelt, Franklin D. Roosevelt, John F. Kennedy, George W. Bush, and Barack Obama.

Roger Williams (right) believed in freedom of religion. When he was banned from Massachusetts, he started the Rhode Island Colony.

In 1635 Williams was put on trial for his beliefs and told to go back to England. But instead Williams traveled south from Massachusetts and formed the Rhode Island Colony. Other like-minded people soon followed.

Time for Celebration and Fun

The Puritans did not allow musical instruments in church. They also didn't celebrate birthdays or even Christmas or Easter. But the Puritans did find time to enjoy themselves.

For Puritans events like weddings, the birth of a baby, and the harvest of crops were reasons to celebrate. These were times to enjoy feasts of salted fish, roasted meat, vegetable stew, pumpkin pie, bread pudding, and apple cider.

The open common area in each town was a place for gathering. People shared news and traded the products they made. They also played a game called "ninepins" that was similar to bowling. Children also played with marbles, tops, and kites.

The American colonists had to work hard just to survive, but they found time to play games, such as "ninepins" or "bowls."

Chapter 4:

Defending a Way of Life

By the mid-1640s, the Massachusetts Bay Colony was home to about 14,000 people. Towns and farms spread across Native American hunting grounds and fishing areas. Colonists' cows trampled the natives' gardens. The colonists even expected tribes to obey the colony's laws instead of their own tribal laws.

Not surprisingly the once-friendly relations between the Massachusetts colonists and Native Americans turned sour. Some frustrated tribes finally turned to violence to drive the English out of the region. But the colonists were prepared. In 1643 several Puritan settlements agreed to help protect each other from Native American attacks. Plymouth, Massachusetts Bay, and two colonies that would later join the Connecticut Colony called themselves the United Colonies of New England.

In 1675 violence erupted into a short but bloody war when Plymouth colonists killed three Wampanoag men accused of murder. Wampanoag Chief Metacomet, also known as King Philip, was furious. In what became known as King Philip's War, Metacomet led several tribes in attacking Colonial towns in Massachusetts, Connecticut, Rhode Island, and Maine.

The United Colonies pulled together an army of more than 1,000 men. In 14 months of war, nearly 2,500 colonists and 5,000 Native Americans, including Chief Metacomet, were killed. Dozens of towns and villages were attacked. Some were destroyed. Many of the surviving Native Americans were captured and sold into slavery.

Enemies Inside the Colony

In 1692 some Puritans began to suspect their own neighbors were performing evil acts. In the town of Salem, many townspeople accused others—mostly women—of practicing witchcraft. As fear swept the town, more than 150 people were accused. Colonial leaders held trials, and 20 people were found guilty of witchcraft. Townspeople watched as the accused were hanged or crushed to death under heavy stones. The governor of Massachusetts put an end to the Salem Witch Trials in 1693, after his own wife was accused.

Sarah Good (1653–1692)

Sarah Good was one of the first victims of the Salem Witch Trials. When her husband died in 1686, he left her in great debt. She then married William Good, but they too struggled to survive. When they lost their home, William, Sarah, and their two children were forced to live on the streets of Salem. William begged or traded work for food and lodging for his family. But many people didn't like Sarah, so the family was unwelcome in many homes.

On February 29, 1692, Sarah Good—along with Sarah Osborne and a slave named Tituba—were charged with witchcraft. Accused of casting spells, they were arrested and put on trial. Sarah Good had no friends in the town to defend her. Even her husband and 6-year-old daughter spoke out against her. But Good insisted, "I am falsely accused!"

Good, Osborne, and Tituba were all found guilty. On high ground overlooking the town, Good and four other women were hanged on July 19, 1692.

A United Colony

In 1691 England combined the Massachusetts Bay and Plymouth Colonies into one colony, which also included parts of present-day Maine and Canada. The king chose a governor for the Massachusetts Colony. This change made Massachusetts the second-largest colony behind Virginia.

By 1700 Boston was the largest city in the American Colonies. Boston was also an important center for trade. Craftsmen in Massachusetts built ships that carried wood, cod, and whale oil to other ports. They returned from England with factory-made clothing and iron stoves. They brought sugar and molasses from the Caribbean.

Boston's Old State House (center) was built in 1713 to house the Colonial government of Massachusetts. Since then, it has witnessed an incredible amount of history.

Slavery in the North

Not long after the Puritans reached Massachusetts, enslaved Africans began to arrive. By 1750 there were 4,000–5,000 slaves in Massachusetts. Soon Boston was a center for the slave trade in America.

Most slaves were people who had been kidnapped in Africa and sold into slavery. Conditions on slave ships were horrible. Hundreds of people were chained to each other and packed together tightly. They could barely move or breathe. Many died on the journey. Those who did survive were sold to slave masters when they reached America.

Unlike enslaved people in the Southern Colonies, many slaves in Massachusetts did not spend their days working in farm fields. Instead they worked as servants, maids, nannies, or cooks in the homes of wealthy colonists. Others trained to learn a trade or skill to become carpenters, tailors, shoemakers, or weavers.

Not everyone agreed with the practice of slavery. Some spoke out or wrote articles against it. In 1700 Samuel Sewall, one of the judges in the Salem Witch Trials, wrote an essay called "The Selling of Joseph." In the essay Sewall spoke out against slavery and the slave trade. "The Selling of Joseph" is considered the first antislavery document in America.

James Otis, Jr. also believed that African-Americans should have the same freedoms, rights, and opportunities as white people. In 1764 he wrote a pamphlet called *The Rights of the British Colonies Asserted and Proved*. In the pamphlet he argued that all colonists—whether slave or free— have the right to life, liberty, and property. He argued that those basic rights come from God, not the government.

James Otis, Jr. was one of the first people to speak out against slavery in America.

> *"The Colonists are by the law of nature free born, as indeed all men are, white or black."*
>
> —James Otis, Jr., *The Rights of the British Colonies Asserted and Proved*, 1764

Chapter 5:
Heading Toward Revolution

Great Britain and France went to war in North America in 1754. Britain and France both wanted to control certain parts of North America. Native American **allies** chose sides and helped fight the French and Indian War (1754–1763). Most of the war's battles took place outside Massachusetts, but men from the colony still fought. They gained valuable experience that would prepare them for a greater war to come.

Trouble with Great Britain

American colonists rejoiced after they helped Great Britain defeat the French in 1763. But the war was expensive, and Great Britain had borrowed money from other countries. **Parliament** decided to tax the colonists on everyday goods. The money from the colonists was used to help pay the debt. In 1764 Parliament passed the Sugar Act. This made sugar arriving in Boston Harbor more expensive for colonists to buy. A year later Parliament passed the Stamp Act. This placed a hefty tax on paper products, such as newspapers and playing cards.

During the French and Indian War, the British and French battled against each other for control of land in North America. Native Americans fought on both sides.

Residents of Boston took to the streets to protest the Stamp Act and other taxes that they felt were unfair.

Resistance and Violence

Frustrated colonists claimed it was not fair for Parliament in faraway England to make laws for the American Colonies. For more than 100 years, the colonists had made their own laws and elected their own leaders. Many of Massachusetts' leading men joined a group called the Sons of Liberty to protest the Stamp Act and other unfair laws. They wrote articles and convinced some people to **boycott** British goods. They also led protests in Boston and burned dummies, called effigies, made to look like British leaders. Some even destroyed the homes and offices of the tax collectors. They hoped their actions would force Britain to put an end to the unfair taxes.

Did You Know?

Famous Bostonians John Hancock, Paul Revere, and Samuel Adams were all members of the Sons of Liberty.

ally—a person or country that helps and supports another
Parliament   Great Britain's lawmaking body
boycott—to refuse to buy or use a product or service to protest something believed to be wrong or unfair

The Stamp Act was **repealed** in 1766, but just a year later, Parliament issued the Townshend Acts. These new taxes applied to a variety of everyday products, including glass, paint, lead, and tea. Fed up with the king and his taxes, many colonists began boycotting all British goods.

Tensions in Boston erupted into further violence in 1770. The city was already full of British soldiers sent to enforce Britain's tax laws. On March 5 frustrated colonists threw snowballs and rocks at some of the British soldiers. The soldiers fired their guns, killing five colonists. News of this "Boston Massacre" enraged **Patriots** throughout the 13 Colonies.

Five American colonists were killed during the Boston Massacre, including Crispus Attucks, a former slave.

Britain tried to soothe the colonists by lifting many of the taxes. Even the hated Townshend Acts were repealed. But the colonists were outraged that the tax on tea remained. At the time the colonists drank nearly 2 million pounds of tea per year.

The colonists were also frustrated that Great Britain taxed them without allowing Colonial representatives to be part of Parliament. They wanted to have a say in the decisions that affected their daily lives. As a result Bostonians refused to drink tea or buy British goods arriving in Boston Harbor.

Samuel Adams (1722–1803)

Samuel Adams was the son of a Boston merchant and bank owner. From an early age, Adams witnessed Parliament's power over the colonists when the British shut down his father's bank.

Adams began serving in the Massachusetts legislature 1765. He also joined the Sons of Liberty. Adams organized a "committee of correspondence" in Boston to send letters to other towns to share news about the problems with Great Britain. Similar committees of correspondence soon formed across the 13 Colonies.

Adams was skillful at inspiring people to join the Patriots' cause. He organized protests and public demonstrations in favor of America's independence. He also signed the Declaration of Independence. He later served as governor of Massachusetts from 1794 to 1797.

repleal—to officially cancel something, such as a law
Patriot—a person who sided with the colonies during the Revolutionary War

Destruction in the Harbor

On December 16, 1773, Boston's Sons of Liberty staged an event that Great Britain found unforgivable. At least 50 colonists disguised as Native Americans raided three British ships in Boston Harbor. They dumped 340 chests of tea into the water. This event became known as the Boston Tea Party.

Following the Boston Tea Party, the British passed stricter laws to punish the people of Massachusetts. The colonists referred to them as the "Intolerable Acts." These acts placed a British military general in charge of Massachusetts' government. British naval ships also blocked trade in Boston Harbor until the city paid for the destroyed tea. The colonists were even forced to let British soldiers stay in their homes.

Inching Closer to War

Although the Intolerable Acts applied mainly to Massachusetts, people in the other colonies worried that the British would punish them in the same way. As a result representatives from the 13 Colonies decided to work together to force the British to treat them fairly.

During the Boston Tea Party, colonists threw 46 tons of tea into Boston Harbor. That much tea would be worth more than $2 million today.

Realizing their problems with Great Britain could not be resolved peacefully, the colonists began talking about forming their own independent nation. In September and October 1774, representatives from 12 of the 13 Colonies met at the First Continental Congress in Philadelphia. (Georgia did not take part.)

Some of the representatives were wealthy farmers from the Southern Colonies. Many of them wanted to make peace with Great Britain. But others, like cousins John and Samuel Adams, argued that the colonies needed to be firm with Britain. Congress sent King George III the Declaration of Resolves— a list of complaints and the rights they felt Americans deserved. They also organized a formal boycott of all British goods in the American Colonies until the king addressed their complaints.

John Adams (1735–1826)

John Adams had a deep connection to his home state of Massachusetts. Born in Quincy on October 30, 1735, his ancestors were Puritans who arrived in the early years of the Massachusetts Bay Colony. His father was a farmer, a religious leader, and a member of the town government.

Adams studied law at Harvard University. Like many others, he found the Stamp Act of 1765 to be unacceptable. He protested by writing newspaper articles claiming that the taxes violated the colonists' basic rights.

Adams strongly believed that the colonies should be free of British rule. During the Revolutionary War, Adams worked tirelessly getting supplies for the Continental army. He also served on 90 committees as a member of Congress.

Adams helped work out the terms of the Treaty of Paris, which formally ended the Revolutionary War. He became George Washington's vice president in 1789 and was elected president in 1796. John Adams died in Massachusetts on July 4, 1826, the same day that Thomas Jefferson died in Virginia. It was the 50th anniversary of the adoption of the Declaration of Independence, which was written by Jefferson with some help from Adams.

Chapter 6:
War and Independence

When King George III refused to address the colonists' complaints, the Americans felt ignored and disrespected. They no longer wanted to compromise with the king. They wanted freedom and independence from Great Britain, and they were ready to go to war to get it.

In early 1775 word got back to England that the colonists were preparing for war. In April British General Thomas Gage led his troops out of Boston to capture American weapons and gunpowder. But Paul Revere, a **silversmith** from Boston, rode all night to warn colonists that the British were on the move.

On April 19 red-coated British soldiers arrived on a field in Lexington, Massachusetts. Thanks to the warning, a small Patriot **militia** was waiting for them. They were known as "minutemen" because they were prepared to defend their town at a moment's notice. Yet these colonists were greatly outnumbered. Fewer than 80 Patriots faced around 700 British soldiers.

Paul Revere let colonists know that the British were on their way to Lexington.

It is unclear who fired the first shot, but in a cloud of musket fire, the Revolutionary War had begun. When the smoke cleared, eight Patriots were dead, and the British marched toward the town of Concord. While the British were searching for American weapons and supplies, about 2,000 colonists arrived on the scene. Hearing the news of the battle at Lexington, they had grabbed their weapons and prepared to join the fight.

The British were better trained and well armed, but now *they* were outnumbered. As minutemen continued to arrive by the dozens, the British had no choice but to retreat. At the end of the day, about 90 colonists were dead, wounded, or missing, while the British suffered about 300 casualties.

A group of minutemen held back the British as they attempted to cross the Concord Bridge on April 19, 1775.

silversmith—a person who makes items out of silver

militia—a group of volunteer citizens who are organized to fight but are not professional soldiers

The Death of General Warren at the Battle of Bunker's Hill, 17 June 1775 was painted by artist John Trumbull, who was at the battle. Warren—a popular doctor and politician—was one of the first people killed during the Revolutionary War.

The Struggle for Boston

Following the Battles of Lexington and Concord, Great Britain tightened its control over Boston. The Patriots watched as Boston Harbor was swarmed by British warships carrying additional soldiers and weapons.

On the night of June 16, 1775, about 1,000 Patriots were ordered to guard Bunker Hill, a ridge on Boston's north side. But in the dark, they passed Bunker Hill and instead spent the night nearby on Breed's Hill. They positioned themselves behind large rocks and mounds of dirt and waited for the British to strike.

The next morning the British stormed the hill. But with little gunpowder for their muskets, the Patriots were told not to fire until the **Redcoats** were close. When the Patriots opened fire, the British quickly retreated. The British regrouped and fought until the Patriots ran out of gunpowder and were forced into hand-to-hand combat. During the Battle of Bunker Hill, as it was called, more than 1,000 Redcoats were killed or wounded. The Americans lost 400 in what would prove to be the bloodiest battle of the Revolutionary War.

The Battle of Dorchester Heights

For months following the Battle of Bunker Hill, the British and Patriots struggled for control of Boston. Then Boston-born Henry Knox suggested a plan to George Washington, the commander in chief of the Continental army. Knox made a risky journey from Boston to Fort Ticonderoga in New York to retrieve more than 50 pieces of **artillery**, including several cannons. During a heavy snowstorm, Knox and his men covered nearly 700 miles round-trip transporting the weapons to Boston on boats and sleds.

Under cover of darkness during the night of March 4, 1776, the Americans positioned the newly acquired weapons on Dorchester Heights, overlooking Boston Harbor. When the British awoke the next morning to find the guns pointing down at them, they were shocked. British General William Howe ordered his troops to attack, but a terrible storm ruined his plans. Realizing their defeat, the British left Boston on March 17.

George Washington at Dorchester Heights

> *"My God! These fellows have done more work in one night than I could make my army do in three months."*
>
> —British General William Howe, March 5, 1776, upon seeing the American weapons positioned on Dorchester Heights

Redcoats—a nickname for British soldiers, named after the color of their uniforms

artillery—cannons and other large guns used during battles

Fighting for Independence

In the spring of 1776, the Continental Congress met again to make some important decisions. Representatives from the 13 Colonies discussed whether or not to break ties with Britain. Some colonies weren't convinced that breaking away from the parent country was the right thing to do. Others, like Massachusetts, were eager for independence.

With help from John Adams and Benjamin Franklin, Thomas Jefferson wrote the Declaration of Independence. Congress approved the document on July 4, 1776. In Boston the Declaration of Independence was read from the balcony of the Old State House on July 18. Statues representing British rule were pulled off the building's roof and destroyed.

The War Moves South

In the fall of 1777, the British lost an important battle near Saratoga, New York. With that the tide began to turn in favor of the Americans, and the British decided to focus their attention on the Southern Colonies. The British felt it would be easier to win colonists' support—and therefore battles—in the South because more **Loyalists** lived there.

Critical Thinking with Primary Sources

John Adams was the main author of the Massachusetts Constitution of 1780. How do the words shown in Article I of this constitution reflect the ideas that the Patriots were fighting for during the Revolutionary War? In the early 1780s, two slaves in Massachusetts used this document in court to sue for their freedom. They won their freedom, and Massachusetts outlawed slavery in 1783. Which ideas in this passage do you think they might have used to argue for their freedom?

[7]

PART the First.

A DECLARATION of the RIGHTS of the Inhabitants of the Commonwealth of MASSACHUSETTS.

Art. I. ALL men are born free and equal, and have certain natural, essential, and unalienable rights ; among which may be reckoned the right of enjoying and defending their lives and liberties ; that of acquiring, possessing, and protecting property ; in fine, that of seeking and obtaining their safety and happiness.

The British captured Savannah, Georgia, and Charles Town, South Carolina. Then in 1780 British Major General Charles Cornwallis began moving his troops north into the Carolinas and Virginia. But Major General Nathanael Greene tricked Cornwallis and his troops into chasing the Patriots all over the Carolinas and then into Virginia.

Cornwallis and his soldiers arrived in Yorktown, Virginia, in August 1781. While waiting for **reinforcements**, they spent several weeks building defensive **fortifications**. By October, Cornwallis and his men were exhausted and running out of supplies. They were also outnumbered by Washington's men nearly two to one.

At the Battle of Yorktown, the Continental army knocked down the British Army's fortifications and charged up a hill to attack the Redcoats.

When the Battle of Yorktown began on October 9, the Continental army overpowered the British with cannonballs and gunfire. On October 19, Cornwallis had no choice but to surrender. It was the last major battle of the Revolutionary War. The Americans had won their independence!

British and American representatives signed the Treaty of Paris on September 3, 1783. With this peace treaty, Great Britain officially recognized the United States of America as an independent nation.

Loyalist—a colonist who was loyal to Great Britain during the Revolutionary War

reinforcements—additional troops sent into battle

fortification—a structure (such as a wall or tower) that is built to protect a place

Another Rebellion Erupts

After the war Massachusetts had serious money problems. It owed money to men who fought in the war and to merchants who had provided supplies. The Massachusetts government raised money by forcing everyone to pay a tax. But many poor farmers could not afford to pay the tax, so they lost their farms. Some even went to prison.

In 1786 a farmer and Revolutionary War veteran named Daniel Shays led angry farmers throughout Massachusetts to protest the taxes. Many of the farmers were also veterans, and they felt betrayed. They had risked their lives fighting for independence, and then they lost their farms to pay for it.

Shays and his followers—which sometimes numbered more than 1,500 men—held protests to block the taxes from being collected. Congress was bound by the Articles of Confederation, the law of the land and could offer no help in stopping the rebellion. In order to stop Shays and his rebels, the governor of Massachusetts had to borrow money from merchants to hire militiamen.

In January 1787 Shays and his men planned a raid in Springfield to steal weapons. But 1,200 militiamen were waiting for them. When the militiamen opened fire, four of Shays' men were killed and 20 were wounded. The rebels retreated, and Shays' Rebellion was over.

Militiamen from Massachusetts attacked Daniel Shays and his followers, preventing them from raiding a weapons storehouse.

From Colony to State

Shays' Rebellion showed Americans that their current system of government was too weak. Such concerns led to the writing of the U.S. Constitution in 1787.

On February 6, 1788, Massachusetts became the sixth state when it **ratified** the U.S. Constitution. Boston was chosen as the state capital.

Boston has fulfilled John Winthrop's dream of a special "city on a hill." Today the city is full of universities and tall office buildings that overlook a busy harbor. Visitors can travel the Freedom Trail around the city to learn about the people and places that launched a revolution and inspired ideas Americans still live by today.

Now surrounded by modern buildings and skyscrapers, Boston's Old State House continues to be a symbol of America's freedom and independence.

> *"If government shrinks, or is unable to enforce its laws; fresh maneuvers will be displayed by the insurgents ... and every thing will be turned topsy turvey in that State ..."*
>
> —George Washington, February 3, 1787, in a letter to Henry Knox upon hearing of Shays' Rebellion

ratify—to formally approve a document

Timeline

1607 Virginia, the first permanent English colony in North America, is established.

1620 A group of about 120 Pilgrims travel to America on the *Mayflower*. They establish Plymouth Colony.

1621 The Pilgrims celebrate the first Thanksgiving feast with their Wampanoag allies. William Bradford is elected governor of the Plymouth Colony.

1629 King James I gives permission for the Massachusetts Bay Company to establish a colony in North America.

1630 John Winthrop and a group of Puritans settle the city of Boston.

1632 Boston becomes the capital of the Massachusetts Bay Colony.

1634 Puritans purchase the land now known as the Boston Common. In the 1830s Boston Common becomes America's first public park.

1635 The Boston Latin School is established in Boston. It was America's first public school.

1636 Harvard University is founded near Boston, in present-day Cambridge. It is the oldest college in the United States.

1643 When Dutch and Native American forces threaten the Puritan colonies, the colonies join together as the United Colonies of New England.

1675 Colonists and Native Americans battle in King Philip's War, which ends the following year.

1691 The Plymouth and Massachusetts Bay Colonies and parts of present-day Maine and Canada combine to form the Massachusetts Colony.

1692 The Salem Witch Trials begin.

1770 British soldiers kill five colonists during the Boston Massacre.

1773 During what became known as the Boston Tea Party, colonists dump 340 chests (46 tons) of British tea into Boston Harbor.

1775 British soldiers and armed colonists fight the first battles of the Revolutionary War in Lexington and Concord, Massachusetts.

1776 In March Colonial soldiers defeat British troops at Dorchester Heights, forcing the British to leave Boston. In July the Declaration of Independence is adopted.

1780 John Adams writes the Massachusetts Constitution. John Hancock is elected the first governor of Massachusetts.

1783 The Treaty of Paris is signed, formally ending the Revolutionary War.

1786 Daniel Shays leads farmers in a rebellion against the Massachusetts government. It ends the next year.

1788 Massachusetts ratifies the U.S. Constitution and becomes the sixth state to join the United States.

Glossary

ally (AL-eye)—a person or country that helps and supports another

ancestor (AN-ses-tur)—a family member who lived a long time ago

Anglican (AN-gli-kuhn)—relating to the Church of England

artillery (ahr-TIL-ur-ee)—cannons and other large guns used during battles

boycott (BOY-kot)—to refuse to buy or use a product or service to protest something believed to be wrong or unfair

charter (CHAR-tuhr)—an official document granting permission to set up a new colony, organization, or company

colonize (KAH-luh-nize)—to formally settle a new territory

council (KOUN-suhl)—a group of people elected to make decisions for a larger group

delegate (DEL-uh-guht)—someone who represents other people at a meeting

fertilizer (FUHR-tuh-ly-zuhr)—a substance added to soil to make crops grow better

fortification (FOR-tuh-fi-kay-shun)—a structure (such as a wall or tower) that is built to protect a place

immigrant (IM-uh-gruhnt)—a person who moves from one country to live permanently in another

Loyalist (LOI-uh-list)—a colonist who was loyal to Great Britain during the Revolutionary War

militia (muh-LISH-uh)—a group of volunteer citizens who are organized to fight but are not professional soldiers

natural resource (NACH-ur-uhl REE-sorss)—something in nature that people use, such as coal and trees

Parliament (PAR-luh-muhnt)—Great Britain's lawmaking body

Patriot (PAY-tree-uht)—a person who sided with the colonies during the Revolutionary War

pillory (PIL-uh-ree)—a device formerly used for publicly punishing wrongdoers consisting of a wooden frame with holes in which the head and hands can be locked

Puritan (PYOOR-uh-tuhn)—a follower of a strict religion common during the 1500s and 1600s. Puritans wanted simple church services and enforced a strict moral code.

ratify (RAT-uh-fye)—to formally approve a document

Redcoats (RED-kohts)—a nickname for British soldiers, named after the color of their uniforms

reinforcements (ree-in-FORSS-muhnts)—additional troops sent into battle

repeal (ri-PEEL)—to officially cancel something, such as a law

silversmith (SIL-vur-smith)—a person who makes items out of silver

smallpox (SMAWL-poks)—a disease that spreads easily from person to person, causing chills, fever, and pimples that scar

Critical Thinking Using the Common Core

1. How did Native Americans help colonists survive? Use ideas from the text to support your answer. (Key Ideas and Details)

2. Unlike Continental soldiers and militia, British soldiers were professionally trained and well armed. But what gave Americans the advantage in places like Concord and Dorchester Heights? (Integration of Knowledge and Ideas)

3. In the Massachusetts Constitution of 1780, John Adams used the words "liberty" and "property." Why were these words so important to colonists? Use examples from the book and what you know about America's Colonial history to support your answer. (Integration of Knowledge and Ideas)

Read More

Barber, Nicola. *Who Journeyed on the* Mayflower? Primary Source Detectives. Chicago: Heinemann Library, 2014.

Doeden, Matt. *The Salem Witch Trials: An Interactive History Adventure*. You Choose Books. North Mankato, Minn.: Capstone Press, 2011.

Holub, Joan. *What Was the First Thanksgiving?* What Was ...? New York: Grosset & Dunlap, 2013.

Internet Sites

FactHound offers a safe, fun way to find Internet sites related to this book. All of the sites on FactHound have been researched by our staff.
Here's all you do:
Visit *www.facthound.com*
Type in this code: 9781515722373

Check out projects, games and lots more at
www.capstonekids.com

Source Notes

Page 15, primary source box: "Mayflower Compact: 1620." *The Avalon Project: Documents in Law, History and Diplomacy.* Yale Law School: Lillian Goldman Law Library. Accessed April 27, 2016. http://avalon.law.yale.edu/17th_century/mayflower.asp.

Page 17, callout quote: John Winthrop, "A Model of Christian Charity, 1630," *The Winthrop Society.* Accessed April 27, 2016. http://winthropsociety.com/doc_charity.php.

Page 25, sidebar, line 24: Ezekiell Chevers, "Examination of Sarah Good," *Salem Witch Trials: Documentary Archive and Transcription Project.* Accessed April 27, 2016. http://salem.lib.virginia.edu/texts/tei/swp?div_id=n63.

Page 27, callout quote: James Otis. *The Rights of the British Colonies Asserted and Proved.* Boston: 1765, p. 43. Accessed April 27, 2016. https://archive.org/stream/cihm_20373#page/n47/mode/2up/search/white+or+black.

Page 37, callout quote: David McCullough. *1776.* New York: Simon & Schuster, 2005, p. 93.

Page 39, primary souce box: "Constitution of the Commonwealth of Massachusetts." *Massachusetts Court System.* Accessed April 27, 2016. http://www.mass.gov/courts/court-info/sjc/edu-res-center/jn-adams/mass-constitution-1-gen.html#TheMassachusettsConstitution.

Page 41, callout quote: George Washington. "From George Washington to Henry Knox, 3 February 1787," *Founders Online, National Archives.* Accessed April 27, 2016. http://founders.archives.gov/documents/Washington/04-05-02-0006.

Did You Know?

Boston is nicknamed "Beantown" because in Colonial times, a popular meal was beans baked and sweetened with molasses. On Saturdays, Puritan women cooked these Boston baked beans for Sunday's family meals.

Select Bibliography

Blumberg, Jess. "A Brief History of the Salem Witch Trials." *Smithsonian*. October 23, 2007. Accessed May 16, 2016. http://www.smithsonianmag.com/history/a-brief-history-of-the-salem-witch-trials-175162489/?no-ist.

Borneman, Walter R. *American Spring: Lexington, Concord, and the Road to Revolution*. Boston: Little Brown, 2014.

Doherty, Kieran. *William Bradford: Rock of Plymouth*. Brookfield, Connecticut: Twenty-First Century Books, 1999.

Drake, Samuel Gardner. *The History and Antiquities of the City of Boston: From Its Settlement in 1630 to the Year 1670*. Boston. L. Stevens, 1854.

Howe, Daniel Wait. *The Puritan Republic of the Massachusetts Bay in New England*. Massachusetts: Bowen-Merrill, 1899.

Lindenauer, Leslie J. "Massachusetts Bay Colony." *Dictionary of American History*. Ed. Stanley I. Kutler. 3rd ed. Vol. 5. New York: Charles Scribner's Sons, 2003.

Simmons, Richard C. *The American Colonies: From Settlement to Independence*. New York: W.W. Norton & Company, 1981.

Smith, Jennifer. "Event Notes Boston's History of Slavery." *The Boston Globe*. August 23, 2015. Accessed May 16, 2016. https://www.bostonglobe.com/metro/2015/08/23/boston-history-slavery-remembered/lWDkhBD6ilLvdcrgsy3jeL/story.html.

Smith, Tom, John S. Bowman and Maurice Isserman. *Discovery of the Americas, 1492–1800*. New York: Infobase Publishing, 2009.

Wiencek, Henry. *Southern New England*. The Smithsonian Guides to Historic America. Stewart, Tabori & Chang: New York, 1989.

Regions of the 13 Colonies

Northern Colonies	Middle Colonies	Southern Colonies
Connecticut, Massachusetts, New Hampshire, Rhode Island	Delaware, New Jersey, New York, Pennsylvania	Georgia, Maryland, North Carolina, South Carolina, Virginia
land more suitable for hunting than farming; trees cut down for lumber; trapped wild animals for their meat and fur; fished in rivers, lakes, and ocean	The "Breadbasket" colonies—rich farmland, perfect for growing wheat, corn, rye, and other grains	soil better for growing tobacco, rice, and indigo; crops grown on huge farms called plantations; landowners depended heavily on servants and slaves to work in the fields

Index